NEST OF THISTLES

Other volumes in the series:

Eve Names the Animals by Susan Donnelly (selected by Anthony Hecht)
Rain by William Carpenter (selected by Maxine Kumin)
This Body of Silk by Sue Ellen Thompson (selected by X. J. Kennedy)
Valentino's Hair by Yvonne Sapia (selected by Donald Hall)
The Holyoke by Frank Gaspar (selected by Mary Oliver)
Dangerous Life by Lucia Perillo (selected by Peter Davison)
Bright Moves by J. Allyn Rosser (selected by Charles Simic)
The House Sails Out of Sight of Home by George Mills (selected by Philip Booth)
In the Blood by Carl Phillips (selected by Rachel Hadas)
The Eighth Continent by Don Boes (selected by A. R. Ammons)
Plums & Ashes by David Moolten (selected by David Ferry)
Living at the Epicenter by Allison Funk (selected by Sonia Sanchez)
Understory by Michelle Boisseau (selected by Molly Peacock)
Reading the Water by Charles Harper Webb (selected by Edward Hirsch)
American Spirituals by Jeffrey Greene (selected by Carolyn Kizer)
Walking Liberty by James Haug (selected by Alfred Corn)
The Drowned City by Jennifer Atkinson (selected by Carl Phillips)
Bullroarer: A Sequence by Ted Genoways (selected by Marilyn Hacker)
All the Blood Tethers by Catherine Sasanov (selected by Rosanna Warren)
The Actual Moon, The Actual Stars by Chris Forhan (Selected by Robert Cording)
Beautiful Motion by Dana Roeser (Selected by Ellen Bryant Voigt)

The Morse Poetry Prize
Edited by Guy Rotella

18 August 2008

Annie Boutelle [signature]

ANNIE BOUTELLE

Nest of Thistles

THE 2005 MORSE POETRY PRIZE

Selected and Introduced by Eric Pankey

*For Cicely —
What a pleasure
to meet you!
Love,
Annie.*

Northeastern University Press
BOSTON
Published by University Press of New England
Hanover and London

Northeastern University Press

Published by University Press of New England,

One Court Street, Lebanon, NH 03766

www.upne.com

© 2005 by Annie Boutelle

Printed in the United States of America

5 4 3 2 1

The author gratefully acknowledges permission to reprint excerpts from the following:

"The Purse-Seiner Atlantis," from *Rooms Are Never Finished* by Agha Shahid Ali. Copyright
© 2002 by Agha Shahid Ali. Used by permission of W. W. Norton & Company, Inc.

Hugh MacDiarmid, "The Little White Rose," *The Complete Poems of Hugh MacDiarmid:
Flowers a la Carte,* Carcanet Press Limited, 1993; and "The Little White Rose" by Hugh
MacDiarmid, from *Selected Poetry,* copyright © 1992 by Alan Riach and Michael Grieve,
reprinted by permission of New Directions Publishing Corporation.

Library of Congress Cataloging-in-Publication Data
Boutelle, Annie, 1943–
  Nest of thistles / Annie Boutelle ; selected and introduced by Eric Pankey.
    p. cm. — (The 2005 Morse Poetry Prize)
  ISBN-13: 978-1-55553-647-3 (alk. paper)
  ISBN-10: 1-55553-647-6 (alk. paper)
  ISBN-13: 978-1-55553-648-0 (pbk. : alk. paper)
  ISBN-10: 1-55553-648-4 (pbk. : alk. paper)
  I. Pankey, Eric, 1959– II. Title. III. Morse Poetry Prize ; 2005.
  PS3602.O893N47 2005
  811'.6—dc22   2005012223

for Sheena,

sweet sister

Contents

Song

Acknowledgments

The author gratefully acknowledges the editors of the journals in which these poems first appeared:

Barrow Street: "Ash"
Catamaran: "19 July 2003"
Ekphrasis: "The Greatcoat"
The Georgia Review: "Wanting to Write Like Merwin"
Green Mountains Review: "Bens," "Ghost"
The Hudson Review: "Ancestor Theory"
Iris: "Heureux"
The Massachusetts Review: "'From a Childhood,'" "'I Love You, Darkness,'" "Bridge Street Cemetery"
Manhattan Review : "The Lover"
Metamorphoses: "'Little Year of the Vine,'" "'Orpheus. Eurydice. Hermes'"
Nimrod: "Rockfield Primary School"
Painted Bride: "'Leda,'" "'Washing the Corpse'"
Poet Lore: "One Way to Varanasi," "Poise"
The Red Wheelbarrow: "Bronze Age," "Departure," "Song for My Mother," "Words," "Written on a Leaf"
The Squaw Valley Review: "Child"
The Worcester Review: "Varanasi Morning"

"Witchhazel in March" appeared in *Ars Botanica* (Wallingford, Penn.: ELM Press, 2004).

A sabbatical from Smith College provided dreaming time; Susan Kan taught me how to organize a manuscript; and the critique-group ladies—Amy Dryansky, Marsha Janson, Mary A. Koncel, Margaret Szumowski, and Ellen Doré Watson—gave me courage.

Introduction

In his 1966 essay "Poetry and Happiness," Richard Wilbur argues that the poet, in the making of the poem, is possessed by twin desires. The first is the desire to feel, praise, and "lay claim to as much of the world as possible through uttering the names of things" and thereby to convey "an articulate relishing and mastery of phenomena in general." The second desire of the poet, Wilbur says, beyond "the inventory of external reality," is the "discovery and projection . . . , the exploration and declaration of the self." In Annie Boutelle's *Nest of Thistles*, we find a poet whose poems are charged with the high voltage of these twin desires.

Boutelle's eye for the revelatory detail, her ear for a craggy consonance and airy assonance, and her mind with its well-honed intelligence reveal and explore the self, in particular a self wrought from history, myth, and tradition. Line by line, her "articulate relishing and mastery of phenomena in general" make a corporeal and tangible world out of the strata of yesterdays, as in the book's opening poem, "Bens":

> . . . granite heaved
>
> up and weathered down to what remains. Nothing more
> Scottish than these—their inflexibility, their indifference.
>
> They condemn pretension, and kill fools. Sleeping
> monsters, these whales of hills have traveled
>
> far and plan to go no farther. Cliff, screes, ridges, flints,
> ramparts, boulders, gullies. Such flanks, such haunches, . . .

Rainer Maria Rilke, a poet Boutelle has translated and whose poems she has woven throughout *Nest of Thistles*, says that poems are not about feelings, but things felt. Boutelle wrings from words not only the thing seen but the thing felt and experienced. She inventories and illuminates. A prose poem, "Rockfield Primary School," presents a narrative of flashes and fragments. Boutelle makes the poem wholly from a catalog of memory shards, as the poem's ending reveals:

> If you fall and skin your knee, the janitor pours dettol and water into a bowl and sloshes the stinging mixture on your wound. Miss Mac Intyre was mad about poetry. *O, young Lochinvar has come out of the west.* Her arm soared upward with the beat. In March a diamond blazed on her finger. In April, diamondless, she fled the room. When the Queen is crowned, they give you a gold-crested mug and an orange. Miss MacFadzean kept her belt in her desk and removed it often. There is a hole in the iron gate through which only the thinnest girl can squeeze.

Boutelle returns her reader again and again to the things of this world, to the gnosis embodied in the ephemeral and in those things measured in geologic and mythic time. Nonetheless, the self is the central subject for this writer. She writes to declare, discover, explore, and project the self by way of the ethnographic and the cartographic. She manages, as Robert Duncan said poetry does, to "arouse in contemporary consciousness reverberations of the old myth, to prepare the ground so that when we return we will see our modern texts charged with a plot that had already begun before the first signs and signatures . . . worked upon the walls of Altamira."

Throughout *Nest of Thistles* one is moved by the exilic and elegiac distance of home. *Nest of Thistles* locates itself primarily in Scotland, from where Boutelle emigrated. If the book is nostalgic, it is not a nostalgia flawed by a failure of feeling, but the nostalgia we find in Homer and Sophocles, a homesickness experienced through all the senses and tempered only by story and song. In the poem "Bronze Age," which is subtitled "South Uist, 1500 BCE," the poet speaks through the voice of a woman preserved and transmuted by a bog burial. From the distance of the Hebrides archipelago, she speaks to us:

> Sew my eyes shut, dip me in peat, and let my hair
> still grow. Let the seeds in my intestine rest
> undigested, ready to begin again. Watch nails
> curve long and dangerous. See breasts shrivel.
> I have no vanity to slow the process down.
> Pickle me in salt like herring. Dry me in wind
> or fire. . . .

There is no rest on the journey toward home. The dormant seed will "begin again"; the body goes on as a body, held and changed by death and earth. There is no end even at the end, as the voice continues:

> . . . wrap me
> in fern and deerskin. Lower me into the stone
> house whose six stout walls give shelter. Plunge
> me into silence: it has waited so long it has
> grown tired of waiting. Try not to find me.

In these beautifully made lyric poems the self is wed to place. Only through the mapping of place, through the naming of all that is ordinary and uncanny can the poet begin to survey and explore the intimate distance of a self:

> When did I forget how to plowter, how
> to be scunnert, how to look for foozle
>
> under the bed? When, afraid of sounding
> twee, did I stop saying wee? Who snatched
>
> away douce and douchty? I lost my spurtle, . . .
> ("Words")

Nest of Thistles offers poems that are rigorous and precise, entangled always in memory, in the drama of the world as it is, in the world as we remember it, and in the words into which we have translated it:

> Nuala sees her
> language as a boat, a coracle to launch
>
> in the bulrushes and send off to "some
> Pharaoh's daughter." I saw mine as
>
> something like a wart, a fart, a sneeze.
> And, oh my lost darlings, I run after you
>
> now, wrap treacherous arms round
> you, dust you off, feed you kippers
>
> from Loch Fyne and whisky from Islay,
> then pin you on the page, as witness.
>   ("Words")

ERIC PANKEY

Thistles

Bens

I see them in dreams, Ben More, Stobinian, Nevis, Schiehallion.
Bald and stern, no touch to soften or gentle, granite heaved

up and weathered down to what remains. Nothing more
Scottish than these—their inflexibility, their indifference.

They condemn pretension, and kill fools. Sleeping
monsters, these whales of hills have traveled

far and plan to go no farther. Cliffs, screes, ridges, flints,
ramparts, boulders, gullies. Such flanks, such haunches,

such wide breasts with nipples of cairns that point to heaven
as if a godlike child might reach down his lips and suck. Wind

wraps them in lamentation. Sun polishes their stubbornness.
Moon's silver calls to the silver of their calm. Rain lashes

and lashes them and they do not deign to notice. And children,
looking up, see another kind of parent, one that endures.

Witch Hazel in March

The fierceness of how it hurls
itself toward what's out there,
how it unspools ochre petal-ribbons
to seek the quickest route away
from the star-anise shield at the center
of each bud and the four gilded
arrows that point to the source
of what claims you. This perfume
seizes, drags you to worship
in the snow, to bow before
a sweetness won by centuries
of Chinese gardeners who bent
and fussed and braided love
into the notched stem. It comes
in a flare of ecstasy that orders
you to pour incense on the wind
and drop from body into honeyed air.

Visitants

My dead brother arrives in a rattle
of branches or a glazed road, his eyes

dark mischief under the fringe
of hair, his monkey-creased hand

on my shoulder, arms banging
a welcome to the minnows that roll

in the tide of our embrace.
                      My dead

sister slips between thumb
and forefinger, slice of light,

onion-skin, unheard note, milk
drop, poppy seed, pore.

                    My dead
father crashes through drums

and bagpipes, all those keening
women, trapezes, hunched lions,

waterfalls tireless as rock. Nothing
will stop him. He pushes past

my dead brother and sister, shoves
them into the snow. He has come

so far, and with such pain. He shows
me his feet, toes blue and cracked,

soles torn. I want to give him
mine. I kneel, rub oil into each

bitter crevice. Tomorrow
he'll rampage back for more.

Heathcote

Who packed his clothes?
Her brother has gone to a home.
He can't walk yet.
Did he crawl to Aberdeenshire?
She misses his thick fingers.
Didn't he have a home?
The new baby will live in his room.
No more humming and clapping.
He holds the nurse's hand, stands upright.
The field is wide, the grass tall.
The new baby dies, and he doesn't come back.

Didn't he have a home?
She misses his thick fingers.
The field wide, the grass tall.
Did he crawl to Aberdeenshire?
Who packed his clothes?
He holds the nurse's hand.
He can't walk yet.

Routine

I wasn't yet two but knew that to get
my brother back, I would have swum
the River Tay, hitchhiked to Aberdeenshire.

No one talked of rescue. Shortbread
had to be baked, dogs walked, shoes
polished, while wind heaped sodden

leaves at our door and all the daffodils
turned their heads as we walked by.
Trails the slugs made on the path glistened

disdain. Neighbors hid behind bright windows,
pried open gestures. The bold asked, "And what
do you hear of him?" Even the new baby sister

turned from us, eyes held by the way
the curtain in her room swelled and billowed
with an anguish that couldn't be spoken,

must be held under, choked, sputtering,
a kitten drowning. The sun's fierce light lay
gentle on her cheek, saved its fire for us.

"From a Childhood"

Rainer Maria Rilke's "Aus einer Kindheit"

The room's darkness was riches
to the boy who sat concealed there.
When the mother entered, silent
as a dream, a glass shivered in the quiet
cupboard and she felt the room betraying
her. She kissed the child: "Are you
here?" Both looked anxiously
at the piano: many evenings he had
found himself trapped in her song.

He sat very still. His gaze fixed
on her hand. Weighed down by the ring,
it labored over the white keys as if
struggling in great drifts of snow.

Girl

Flibbertygibbet in the garden, she picked yellow
globes of gooseberries, red globes of currants,
and shoveled them on her tongue. Her sister
caught worms and put them in a jar of black earth
where they spiraled and heaved. The dog licked her
in slobbery joy. The milkman's cart stopped at the gate,
the horse knew whose house came next. Her friend's
grannie lay dead upstairs in a wooden box: her sister
went to see, but she stayed in the kitchen, staring
at the hung-up tawse her friend's father used, thick
leather strips. She rolled plasticene into hard
little balls and sliced them on the edge of an old
tobacco tin: nothing else gave her such satisfaction.
"You're daft, you're daft," she yelled at her sister.
The Polish boy threw stones at her. She swallowed
the sugar cube dunked in the government's cod
liver oil. She drank its sticky orange juice. No
one spoke of her brother, moon-faced, packed off
to Heathcote. She scratched her skin until it bled.

Oban

For I will consider the town of Oban, for it is old and stern and cut from granite, for its houses look with contempt at the sea, for Dr. Johnson slept there on a thin mattress, for fumes from its distillery mix with the salt, for its name means beautiful bay, for fishing boats push through six-foot waves to reach its pier, for in winter George Street is an empty black mirror, for in spring dust and dirt wash into the Black Lynn, for in summer thousands jam its cafés and eat fried haggis, for in autumn slates fly off roofs and hit the unwary, for its virgins are sly, its whores bold, its wives uncertain, its husbands humble, for its children run around MacCaig's Tower and tease cats, for its old women knit lugubrious tales, for its old men rub their mouths before they speak, for knife fights erupt when the pubs close, for behind its prim façade lurk cannabis and ecstasy, for it looks at the islands with nonchalance, for if you can see Mull it's going to rain, and if you can't see Mull it's raining. For thirteen years I ate its bread, I drank its water.

Arrow

Georgia O'Keeffe

"Georgia run the girls"—that's what
the sisters say. And I did. They took
after Mother. Deep down, I'm like

Father, a chip on the water, taking
the waves. When he wanted to see
the country, he just got up and went.

On Sundays we'd take the buggy
to church, the girls in stiff white,
each with a different sash, pink,

green, yellow, blue. I didn't wear
one: I drove, cracking the whip
over the horse's rump, making him fly

down lanes, an arrow that sliced
straight through air to the God
waiting in the clapboard box.

Rockfield Primary School
Oban, 1949–54

In the playground someone gives you a forbidden word so strong
and terrible you can't write it down and so you lose it. Miss Mac-
Gillvary had a highland voice and hair coiled round her head.
Someone's mother brings a piece of bread and jam and hands it
over the wall. Miss Skinner, the fattest teacher, roared so loudly
the building shook. Boys stood dumb before her door—KNOCK
AND ENTER. The girls' toilets are never cleaned: lumps of turd
sprawl on floor and seat. Mrs. Innes was mad about drama. The
Prince in *Snow White* rode a clanking mechanical horse. The
shop near the school sells sweeties in paper bags for threepence
plus a ration coupon. Miss MacPherson gave one girl the choice
of not being excused or being belted: her mother's orders ringing
in her ears, she chose the belt. If you fall and skin your knee, the
janitor pours dettol and water into a bowl and sloshes the sting-
ing mixture on your wound. Miss MacIntyre was mad about po-
etry. *O, young Lochinvar has come out of the west.* Her arm soared
upward with the beat. In March a diamond blazed on her finger.
In April, diamondless, she fled the room. When the Queen is
crowned, they give you a gold-crested mug and an orange. Miss
MacFadzean kept her belt in her desk and removed it often. There
is a hole in the iron gate through which only the thinnest girl can
squeeze.

1952

Kilmacolm

No one told them why they were there, these
two wild girls from the Highlands, whose parents
had waltzed off to Austria, and they didn't like
the town's placid streets or lisping Aunt Eva
or her clean house. Stranded for two weeks,
the elder wept her way through each deliberate
night, salt soaking the sheets as if it planned to run
in long emphatic trickles down the vacuumed
stairs; the younger slept with eyes open and fists
curled. In the pruned and weeded garden, they ate
the tomato sandwiches, bread pink and slimy.
They avoided her stewpot on the back of the stove
where the leftovers bobbed. Only one thing
helped: the tiny plastic cow they bought—
when they filled it and pumped the tail, milk
squirted out the udders. They pumped and
pumped until they thought its back would split.

Mieders

Gray sticks shading into black: obsessively
she sketched each pine tree on the vertiginous
slope, while goat bells chimed and her husband
lay on the double bed in the high-ceilinged
room and his sister lounged on the shady terrace
smoking Pall Malls and drinking sherry. Perhaps
she thought each pencil stroke might save him.
Each a strand in the thick rope she'd toss to the man
making do on one kidney and a cancerous
lung in 90-degree heat. Had she thought the high

mountain air could fix him, or gentians winking
—could they be blue enough?—or wisps of cloud
writing on the sky his passport back to how it was.
He lay in the shuttered room, pretending this
was how it should be—a sister chatting to the nice
woman from Hull, a wife sketching trees, part of him
already falling, no longer there, in that thin air.

"Crucifixion"

Rainer Maria Rilke's "Kreuzigung"

As they were used to herding
wretches to the gallows,
the burly soldiers hung around
and every so often made

faces at the three they'd delivered.
Up there the sorry business of hanging
was happening, and afterwards,
the men were left free to dangle

until a soldier, spattered like a butcher,
said, "This one shouted something."
The centurion looked across from his horse.
"Which one?" He thought he heard

the man call out to Elijah. And they
were all desperate to witness it;
and to prevent the man from dying,
they held the sponge of vinegar

up to his faltering cough, for they hoped
to see the whole play, perhaps even
Elijah. But in the distance Mary shrieked;
and the man howled back, and died.

November

for my father

I've hoarded these scraps: your brother
John, pale freckles speckled his cheeks,
snored on a mattress wedged between
my sister's bed and mine; my mother
placed on your coffin cornflowers
from my patch of garden—did they
tremble in the cold sun?; she read
Para Handy tales to you, your fingers
slack and yellow on the sheet; the night
of your dying, Guy Fawkes fireworks
shattered the sky, then swam to earth.

"Washing the Corpse"

Rainer Maria Rilke's "Leichen-Wäsche"

They had become used to him, but when
the kitchen lamp quivered in the draft,
the unknown man was again wholly
unknown. They washed the neck,

and as they knew nothing of his life,
they made one up, together, while
they washed him. When one of them
coughed, she set the heavy sponge

of vinegar on his face. The other woman
paused too, and drops pattered down
from her hard brush while the convulsed
hand insisted to the entire house
that this man no longer thirsted.

And he proved it. Embarrassed,
they began again, with a short cough,
more hurriedly now, so that, until
they finished the washing, their bent

shadows whirled and writhed on the silent
wallpapered walls, as if caught in a net.
Night in the curtainless window
was merciless. And a nameless man lay
there, bare and clean, and laid down laws.

Family

From that day forth, Death sat at the table,
picking his teeth with a grimy fingernail.

When the mother pegged washing on the line,
Death crouched on her heart and whistled.

When she stirred porridge, he hopped
on her shoulder, poured in extra salt.

Death curled next to each sleeping daughter,
whispered nonsense in each ear, stroked thighs.

He tweaked the cat's whiskers, chased the dog,
let loose the rabbit, turned cartwheels

when the dog came running, fur in its mouth.
Death blew down the chimney, pranced

in the smoke. Each time the mother saw
him, she blanched, but the girls grew used

to him trailing after them, hanging on
as they flew down the hill on their bikes.

He muscled in on everything: birthdays,
menses, kisses. "Boring old Death,"

they muttered. But when Death grew
tired and tried to leave, they told him

to stay. Even the mother knew she'd miss
him, sitting crosslegged there on her heart.

Liminal

How does it come? stalking, like Wyatt's
hart, "with naked foot"; camouflaged
in shadows around Snyder's campfire;
shimmer at the edge, sparking the flickers
that announce migraine; or something softer—
unheard vibration in the ear's canal, wrinkle
on pond surface, something so imperceptible
one perceives, and the body stirs, and heart
and mind swing open to what they recognize:
a nothing, far from language, far from anything
material, an absence that has waited, naked,
relentless, for who knows how many god-
forsaken ages, to find its shape and name:
essence. hint of lemon. sign. sigh. sequel.

Ghost

If I dare, I can find you, still standing at the edge
of the fifties, on our way home from Alyth,
bare-headed, balding, younger now than I. Ford

Pilot warm and regal behind us, wire fence,
wood post, swallows careening over furrows,
amber air, that line of trees. Breath comes

with struggle. Everything moves to the point
when you crouch and offer me the stalks: rye,
corn, whiskered barley. What is this private gift

from father to daughter, from ghost to abandoned
child? Is she to eat the grains, consume their
cunning? Furrows darken into crumbs of earth,

and beyond the treeline wolves race to dens:
He's coming—soon, soon he'll be here. And
still the braided gold trembles on your palm.

The Daughter

Self-appointed guardian of his death:
alsatian, hackles fierce, no rival close.
Not the sister, who talked easily of "Daddy"
while flipping pancakes at the Rayburn.
Nor the grandmother who placed each day
a tight white rose next to his photograph.
Nor the aunt who wore on a thin wrist
his gift of carnelians set in silver. Not,
especially not, the mother, plunging
into mourning, graduating to lavender,
and soaring back to scarlet. Decades
later, she wakes: grandmother and aunt
are ash; mother, femur pinned, drifts
beyond daughter, memory, word. She
imitates her sister, tries out "Daddy,"
flips pancakes, watches the bubbles rise.

Ash

Where is he? Ash scattered on Schiehallion
half a century ago has blown to Vladivostok,

Lima, Hué. Dust under a woman's sole, speck
in the eye, rice shoot rising, plum adangle.

He ate apples in the car, left almost
nothing. Crunched the seeds, the stiff

cartilege that held them in. Passed the stalk
to his girls in the back seat to wonder at.

Crouched down to gut the trout, slicing
the belly, pulling out soft organs, bright

strings and pouches. The loch turned milky
pink. Scales swam on the surface, touched.

Each shoe polished to a high hard shine.
Small to large, lined up. His hands

working the brush, the warmed wax;
pores of leather opened and took it in.

"All serene." And yes, and yes, all
undone, taken in, parceled out,

extricated. Near the citadel
in Hué, a watercress canal.

Nest

Nest of Thistles

More comfy than most folk would jalouse,
fierce prickles to jab the auld enemies
of time and humiliation, down to cushion
the bairns. Wee Willie Winkie coming
ben and a cat singing gray thrums
to the sleeping hen—even the dog spaldered
by the fire disnae gie a cheep. No
bad in times like these. Particularly
if you count the perks: regular delivery
of worms courtesy of the parents, pink
worms of hope, wriggling ones are warmer
than the others, fat black worms of disaster.
Outside a gale spins widdershins and claps
clarty hands, clouds nod defiantly, rain
spits and smirs and sloshes, sneaks
through tight seams, threatens to unsettle
the whole clanjamfrie, but then there's a break
in the weather and a wrinkled moon stravaigs
across the field of stars, pewters each thistle
spear, and clads each thread of down in light.

"I Love You, Darkness"

Rainer Maria Rilke's "Du Dunkelheit, aus der ich stamme"

I love you, darkness from which I rise,
more than fire which circumscribes
the world and carves
a glittering circle
that cuts us off from you.

Darkness embraces everything,
shapes, flames, animals, even me.
It drags us all in,
people and principalities.

It can happen: I sense
a huge force moving closer.

I believe in night.

Births

It was wartime still, you were expected
to suffer, rain hammering on the windows

of the cottage hospital, the road sluiced with it,
blackout scissoring all the light to shreds.

She no longer remembers which one
cost her the tooth. All three were breech,

none what she expected. First the mongol
son, then the normal daughter, then

the one who lived three days.
The first was torture: no one told her

she'd have to bite on a towel. For two
weeks they let her think him normal,

told her only as she packed the suitcase
to go home. She unearthed boulders,

built a fortress round the heart, but
the first daughter started to scale the wall,

and by the time the second was born
there was a tunnel through which the fragile

baby crawled: on the third day, it entered
the chamber, curled there, took up

residence next to a lock of hair, a broken
key, a cap embroidered with thistles.

Passage

After his dying is done, does she fling
open the window to let his soul fly

free? In the old Celtic way, after
struggling to leave, it shouldn't fight

wood and glass, and the opening
of the casement is a last gentle

courtesy. Duncraggan's drafts usher
in a chill current that stirs curtains

and the humid sickroom air. Outside,
Orion strides over Morvern hills, while

Libra calculates a soul's weight and a sickle
moon hunts for new sheaves. A stream

of fishing boats, heading north, passes
the silent red cathedral and the stone

where Fingal tied his dog. Does he look
down, see his daughters tidily asleep

in Angus Cameron's flat, 3 Cawdor
Terrace, all its windows sealed? He can

see without eyes, hear without ears, touch
without fingers. He has left lungs

behind. Is nothing now but space.

Chincherinchees 1960
(Star-of-Bethlehem/ornithogalum thyrsoides)

accept the long slim wooden box don't
think of coffins pry off its lid and save

the stamps you don't know Sharpesville
plunge the stems into a tub of boiling

water watch wax float off close
your eyes to sweat coins tumbling steep

them to the neck in cold water and place
in the cupboard under the stairs how easy

not to see when it's dark as a mine without
diamonds after two days move into light

arrange in crystal next to holly spears
and drops of ignorant blood pristine

petals breathe and keep their silence
ginger&cheese chincherinchees

Memory

"Nothing?" the tarot reader said,
and then, "Oh, honey," compassion
flooding every cranny of her voice.

I was to remember my parents
together—a holiday, at the table,
or beach?—and I could find
no cache of images: no touching
of his shoulder lightly, no
bending to whisper a confidence
in her ear, no giddy laughter
as they walk to Weem or pull
on oars. Instead, I find
her alone, after his death,
climbing a ladder to the high
slate roof, dragging a dinghy
across seaweed rocks, leaning
on a sill to watch lightning flare,
folding eggwhites into silky batter.
She kneels at a picnic fire, urges
flames to catch. Her apron fills
with gooseberries, pale green and hard,
for her to top-and-tail. Her breasts
swing huge and rosy. She never
walks but does a kind of ponytrot
along the Oban street. Once when we
wake to a soft inch of snow, she straps
on skis and zooms downhill to the dentist.

Did death, quick and efficient as the funeral
to which neither daughter was invited,

stroll around the house and gather
up each string that bound him to her?

"Nothing, " I tell her. "Nothing."

Poise

The sea withdrawn and beach now
clear swatch of sand, bolt thrown down,
shimmering sari flinging itself out
upon who knows whose huge table—
how to make, in a poem, a space like
that, sexual and terrible and inviting.
How to pour silence between words,
Vermeer woman with her clay pitcher,
light from the window, bare arm lifted,
poise of everything held. How to fill
the frame so words are weightless
threads, each vowel a balloon tugging
its line, nudging everything that is next
to everything that isn't: salt, sky, sorrow.

Departure

The road glistens with spreadeagled
squirrels, tail plumes waving *au revoir*
as if they greeted death with nonchalance

and grace. My mother had the art:
tucked (five feet, two inches) in her Logan
Airport wheelchair, rolled off to the jetway

by uniformed strangers, her mind
emptying and filling like a harbor washed
by tides, and there was her arm, held high,

her black-gloved hand making those quick
decisive turns to signal *adieu, I'm okay,
so long, see you soon*—as if she was doing

nothing more than taking a gentle stroll
in Pulaski Park before heading back
to the country she came from.

Which Woman

This woman is not my mother.

                Why do you deny her?

This woman moves the white flower next to the teddy bear.

                What would you have her do?

This woman spills crumbs on her chest.

                Why do you care?

This woman holds her teeth in her hand.

                Do you want her to bite the nurse?

This woman cannot walk.

                If she could walk, would you have her run?

This woman's hand looks like my hand.

                Is that so bad?

This woman loves pop music.

                You want Swan Lake?

This woman pats a man's arm.

You want her to live in fear?

This woman says, "Better. Much better."

How do you answer?

Ghazal

How, when the game starts, to ghazal the wind?
How to make salt sweet? to muzzle the wind?

Jacob dreams a ladder, angels on each rung,
a riverbank where he must tussle the wind.

City lost. Street. House. Lover. Can you battle
your way back? Simpler to jostle the wind.

Dust-wrapped infants hold out bones for limbs:
for centuries they've had to nuzzle the wind.

Who speaks from heaven, sweeps human joy
aside, lolls there, admiring his muscle? The wind.

And Annie, seven days at sea, far from Tobermory,
confronts a mackerel sky, tries to puzzle the wind.

Schiehallion

schie: fairy
hallion: Scotland

Island once in seas of ice, quartz
pyramid surveying Rannoch
Moor, Schiehallion's seen plenty.

Hordes clamber up with cellphones
and CD's. The Astronomer Royal
pitched tents and settled in to find earth's

density by measuring how the hill attracts
a pendulum. Here girls in white danced
before Queen Mab, hawthorn and rowan

bobbing in their hair, long green ribbons
twirling. His assistant dreamed away
the time inventing contour lines. Deer

stark on the horizon, their bellowing,
their antler crowns. A woman in kilt
and leather jacket gulped down tears

as she flung her husband's ash: rough
grains blew on her cheek until she learned
to keep the wind behind. Mist slithers

along the ridge, snow sifts into a gully.
Years later, she found some in a pocket,
shook them out, and thought of seeds.

Now bereft of words, she doesn't
think, bobbing cork facing each wave
blankly, anchors aweigh and she's bound

to the hill she can't remember. "Away
with the fairies," the nurse murmurs
in my ear. "She's in her own wee world."

A scar deepens on Schiehallion's flank.
This hunched crone's been so long
coming, it's as if she's always been here.

Conversation

Fiona of the long black hair and motorbike.
("Why did you move to Jura?")
"Love!" Face nothing but grin.

Larks sing as madly going down as up.

The bus jammed with Yanks,
enormous suitcases lurching. "Hauld
on, hen, let them get oot."

Moor constrains. Water leaps toward
salt. Cuckoos don't need cellphones.

"Am just getting masel a cup o tea the noo,"
she yells. Front teeth all gone. Winnie
the Pooh on her backpack. "Orright."

Current silvered, this side of never.

"Ah tell you whaur Ah seen them." "Ah don't
know whaur those two are gone tae." "Mebbe
she's lyin doon." "You need yer high heels on."

Ancestor Theory

They live inside us, spirit parasites whom we ignore.
In the shell of each cell, a hermit crab unafraid to show

its pincers. If we listen, they yell advice, arrange
wild gatherings, quarrel often. Take advantage of any

fever, keep their cooking pots oiled. Weep when we
laugh, curse when we forget. The great-grandfather

in my liver weaves paisley shawls, speaks German,
dances a mean strathspey. A soft-voiced grandmother

lies in my ear, fears mice, smokes Benson & Hedges,
drinks the palest sherry. The grandfather in my toe

hides a marzipan pig in each pocket. He sends out
postcards with scalloped edges: *All well and doing good.*

And the great-great-great-great-great one who nests
in my heart is old beyond age or sex or language,

smallest crab of all, nothing but claws. And my father?
Last glimpsed in 1952, he lies behind one eye, sleeping

a turbulent sleep. And my mother? They're waiting,
for her to find her dancing shoes, for the party to start.

Song for My Mother

Your body is singing, the body that skied,
knelt, wept, climbed Cruachan, rowed boats,
darned socks, scaled ladders, baked girdle
scones, fluffed pillows, pitched tents, opened
to one man, played peekaboo and scrabble,
dug into soil, hauled seaweed, picked harebells,
sneezed, laughed, kissed, tutted disapproval, hiked
Glencoe, birthed three children, buried two,
knitted, cursed, squashed wasps with one brave
thumb, the body that no longer remembers there's
body, that thins to seventy pounds, craves layer
upon layer of sleep. Listen, tiny mother—lullaby
is boat to ferry spirit through air and mist
to the cloud-spun summit of Schiehallion.

Bronze Age

South Uist, 1500 BCE

Sew my eyes shut, dip me in peat, and let my hair
still grow. Let the seeds in my intestine rest
undigested, ready to begin again. Watch nails
curve long and dangerous. See breasts shrivel.
I have no vanity to slow the process down.
Pickle me in salt like herring. Dry me in wind
or fire. Keep me for five hundred years. Prop
me in your sacred place, lay mushroom, oats,
and wine at my black feet. I'll tell you nothing.
Touch my tough skin. Play me your pipes. Chant
me the songs of loss and desire, what wounds
and heals, the braiding and the combing. Place
the jet tenderly round my thin neck, wrap me
in fern and deerskin. Lower me into the stone
house whose six stout walls give shelter. Plunge
me into silence: it has waited so long it has
grown tired of waiting. Try not to find me.

Cradle
for Sheena

How odd to think of all
that is left being so light
so small it fits in a maroon

plastic jar with a screw top.
She would have chosen scarlet.
The jaunty cormorants don't

care, as they ride their waves,
nor the seals, bellies on display,
lounging on the rocks and turning

calm eyes to the boat with the two
black labs, three people, and a jar.
We know it's not really her, you say.

Together we hold it, and the stream
of beige dust flutters. *Goodbye,
Mum.* And I can do nothing

but wipe the rim with my fingers
to free the last grains. You hand
me the bunch of roses and sweet

peas from your garden, and
together we toss it. Buoyant,
tiny, it spins its way down

Loch Linnhe. It rocks
on the gray waves as if
it's found its cradle.

Song

Flowers à la Carte

Via Boston, they stream here
from Holland, Ecuador, Peru.
Star-of-Bethlehem's light erupts
from wheat stalks. Birds
of Paradise, a flock, squawk
orange in the corner. Bamboo
snakes and coils its emerald
frenzy. Rose buds clench.
And I'm longing for bog-cotton
drifts on the moor, yellow orchis
with translucent stems, wiry
stalk of heather, tiny nodding bells.
MacDiarmid refused "the rose
of all the world," chose instead
the "little white rose of Scotland
that smells sharp and sweet—
and breaks the heart." Let wild
hyacinths turn the whole
wood blue. Let primroses
offer their shy gold. Let
thistles hurl purple grief
through tidy suburban
gardens. I want nothing more
than one Grass of Parnassus
plucked from Cruachan's slope,
one star, one burst of white,
one trembling stem.

"The Little Year of the Vine"

excerpts from Rainer Maria Rilke's "Das Kleine Weinjahr"

The memory of snow
vanishes, from one day
to the next, and beige-
blond earth appears.

An eager spade—
listen to it! —strikes—
and you remember green
is the color you prefer.

On the hillside you build
a delicate trellis and stretch out
a hand to the vine, who knows
you and moves toward you.

*

Just as at Saintes-Maries,
in the unspeakable pain there,
when the man who boasts
of being cured tosses
away his crutch and leaves,
so too does the vine leave,
throwing away her scaffold.

So many crutches flung down,
gray on the gray earth—has
the miracle already happened?

And where is the vine? She prances off,
she dances in front of the arches.

Happy are those who follow!

Haggis

Cannonball-size, it sat with its friends
on the marble in the butcher's window.
Despite the myth told to tourists, this

one didn't run maniacally round hills
so its left legs grew longer than its right.
This one grazed on a Kerrera field, next

to reeds and yellow iris. He heard larks
sing and waves slap rock near Horseshoe
Bay. Smelled brine and seaweed. Knew

his mother's call and raced to the teat.
The flock held him safe. He wagged
his long tail, he grew. Then the shifting

ferry to lorry and slaughterhouse,
his stomach soon an inelegant but sturdy
wrap for the "Chieftan o' the Puddin-Race."

We're so proud of this national dare.
Can you eat it? Can you even bear to hear
what's in it? Pepper, oatmeal, onion,

liver, heart. Each Burns Day, my mother
would recite the "Address," increasing
her gusto when she plunged the knife

through skin: "Trenching your gushing
entrails bricht / Like ony ditch; / And then
O what a glorious sicht, / Warm-reekin,

rich." Will likes his fried. Every time
we're in Oban, he gets it from the chip shop,
doused with vinegar and salt, wrapped

in brown paper. He prefers the skin synthetic,
crisp, and swallowed. But this one's the real
Mackay. Steam rises from the slit. Neeps

and tatties cradle it. Here, have a spoonful.
You'll wash it down with Glenlivet. God
knows what you'll see in your dreams.

Wanting to Write Like Merwin

How can I be a Buddhist when I grew up in a house
where silence meant social incompetence.
"Did you hear what the minister said?" "Where
was it we saw the man with the turban?" "Och,
I wouldn't worry." At breakfast, we learned
what everyone dreamed—my mother on a sloop
heading to Ardnamurchan, my father planting
potatoes in the cemetery, my sister attacked
by lobsters, me losing my voice, God knows
about the cat and the dogs, but we speculated.
Oh, to float on silence layered on silence,
great onion rings of silence! And here I sit,
a slow ripening plum, forgetting my grannie's
warning I'll be a long time dead, forgetting
name, face, sorrows, doing nothing but waiting
and listening for tremors, startled thump, whoosh
of the heart, inappropriate gorgeous hiccups.

Handel

At our Water-Music wedding Harry Dobbins
who taught me French and German played
the organ, while outside on the hill leading
down to the bay lurked a former lover, bearded
and professorial, with his new Canadian bride.
I had no clue where I was heading as the aisle
slipped past and I clutched Uncle Angus's steady
arm, but I could see Will's swallowtailed back
and the cowlick I had touched so many times
it felt like mine. I wanted to kneel, Highland
Mary on one bank of a burn, and reach out
dripping hands to my love on the other side—
this troth should be made the ancient sacred
way, in water. When we stepped out, the piper
blew, lover and bride had pulled up stakes.
Atlantic breezes ruffled my lace. We opened
our eyes, dazzled infants, to salt and light.

"Leda"

Rainer Maria Rilke's "Leda"

When his need forced the god to enter
the swan, he was startled by its beauty
and he let himself be confused and slid
into it and the swan carried him forward

before he had a chance to discover
how it felt to be swan. The undone girl
recognized who was coming in the swan
and understood he wanted one thing,

which, even as she resisted, she could
not withhold. It came down low, its neck
pushed past her vague hands, and the god

loosed himself into her, and for the first
time then he took joy in his feathers
and became a real swan inside her.

Heureux

"Heureux," each of my babies
crooned in turn. "Heureux."
None was older than two weeks,
none had been exposed to French;
yet each made that noise in the back
of the throat—sound that sings
of air coming in, going out, harsh
sea-like surge as the hump of tongue
rises, falls, and a wave leaps
from the cycle of lives thrumming
in space and rushes toward us—
each looked me in the eye and said
"heureux" and named our milky
union and the place of language
and the fineness of being
in a world fissured with surprise
and lit with certainty.

The Lover

After her physician ordered
fine-needle aspiration,
she called her new friend
with the melancholy eyes
and asked if he'd come sit
with her. His hand reached
across the café table, cupped
her fingers. She could feel
the slight prickles crossing
from his skin to hers,
ambassadors at a border.

When her physician ordered
surgical biopsy, she went
to her new friend's house, sat
on the pillow of soft green silk.
As she closed eyes and focused
on breath, she opened
to the smell of him, a country
known somewhere, mist-filled
and lost, but recognized now—
the oval cobblestones
glazed with rain, shining
like aubergines, so smooth
and fine were their polished
surfaces—and she wept
for the gift returned to her,
the mist and stones,
the smell of his skin.

When the physician ordered

surgery, she went again
to the room with its high
windows and listened
to the wind blowing the prayer
flags, the fragile slap of fabric
on wood. She slid her hand
to her throat, undid the pearl
buttons, reached for his hand
and placed it on her breast.
It settled there, seabird
alighting on a bollard
at a pier, tucking its wings.

During chemo, she came back
often, knowing they'd be lovers
one way or another, and they lay
for long afternoons, fully clad,
on the futon, a knight and his bald
lady on the hard throne-like bed,
watching the mobile bob
and sway in the space above
their heads as light darted
through the clear windows.

Between radiations, he touched
her intact breast and murmured
of doves, pomegranates,
honey. Her breast became a hill
for children to slide down, a garden
where dark flowers unfurled
fragrances. No one had loved
her breast as this man did,
the tower of its nipple, the pinprick
holes, the shadowy areola. Deep

below the surface, abandoned paths
sang with the patter of hurrying feet.

In the hospital, the nurses knew
to dial his number each morning
at nine. They held the receiver
to her ear so she could hear
his distant voice: "I'm touching
it. My right forefinger is circling
it." On the sixteenth day, he said
he wanted to take the nipple
in his mouth. "I'm your child,"
the voice said. "I've been calling
for you, ceaselessly, combing
each alley, searching each face."

Through the fog of drugs
she feels his lips vibrate
against her skin, and the tide
of white sweetness rises.
"I'm the child of your death,"
he says. "Give it to me. Quick."

Written on a Leaf

Dear Basho, I love the way
you count the holes in the body
and come up with nine, but I need

to remind you that women have
ten and the tenth is not to be
neglected, and oh dear Basho, what

about the inflicted others, piercings
through nipple, eyebrow, tongue?
and the uncountable pores,

miniature doors that fly open
to sweep sweat out and usher
bacteria in? not to mention cavities

of greed and pride, grief, shame,
lust, and the monstrous
caldera of nostalgia ready to toss

up crimson rivers, yards
of gray ash. Maybe counting
isn't the place to begin. Maybe

it's better to sit under the banana
tree and listen for the way wind
brushes against the roof, and feel

how raindrops fall on unsuspecting skin.

Homecoming

The house isn't pink any more, but glows
pale almond, nothing itself, objects tremble
underwater, the couch a striped eel, chair
a crusted rock, bed a sponge, and where
is the cat, more bodies on a Jerusalem
street, and whose taste placed that plaque
of Desdemona next to the lava lamp, paper
scraps (dinner at Apostolis ouzerie, unwritten
card, ferry tickets), Mrs. Krug is dead, and
where do we keep the spoons, the mountain
laurel budded, was the closet always squished,
whose shoes are these, ladybird corpses
weightless on the sill, pebbles from the beach
where Will could have drowned and didn't,
flash floods delay strawberry crop, and does
the Parthenon still sit mellow on its rock?

Unfolding

Next to the indifferent cliff, the four-foot
wings unfold, serene and sure. Rewind

to Diogenes Street, heat pressing down,
courtyard with its lazy turtle and jacarandas,

the chilled museum room. Behind glass
a flute made from bone of an eagle's wing.

Who polished you? Who scooped out the fiber,
drilled the holes? Who dared pry you from the socket?

Later, when he played you at the marriage of his daughter
to the butcher's son, did he regret his hubris and duck

his head, or did he see, for a second, himself as flute
for gods to play, their breath floating you above

Mycenae, guiding his knife, lifting his daughter's
skirts, ruffling his son-in-law's hair, filling the sails

of the boat that will bring him his dark-eyed grandson
and—is this not strange?—his own death in a stream

of notes higher and colder than a human ear can hear.

19 July 2003

for Reetika Vazirani

Green and ochre fields, moss forest. Hudson
a long brown snake beneath the unflappable
bird plowing toward Phoenix. The odd

beauty of houses scrunched tight, each
a shining dot. Algae clogs a pond. Neither she
nor her two-year-old son will see it. No red here.

No lake of blood around them. Locked together,
each a raft on which the other sails. Underground
rivers sprout trees next to fields with circles caught

in squares. She typed Walcott's poems, dreamed
in iambic, lived to write. One green circle burns,
its gray-blue column almost touches the window.

Cumulus towers, whipped-cream reefs. Her hands
trembled as they touched the lectern, the bones
at her wrist clear. She said she had nowhere

to belong till she found poetry. Shadows
of clouds amble, clutch the land, while clouds
race on. Scars on the earth, stripmines, asphalt.

She said she'd buy her first house in Georgia, act
as if she were staying, choose lampshades. Riverbeds
are ferns. Heart winces no. It's like looking at the sun.

"Orpheus. Eurydice. Hermes"

excerpt from Rainer Maria Rilke's "Orpheus. Eurydike. Hermes"

She was inside herself. And being-in-death
filled her completely.
Like a sweet, dark fruit,
she was filled with her own huge death,
so new she understood none of it.

She was in a new virginity, and not
to be disturbed. Her sex folded
in, like a tender flower in the evening,
and her hands, so unused now
to marriage that even the nimble
god's infinitely gentle hand offended
her with its crass intimacy.

She was no longer the fair-haired woman
whom poets praised, no longer
the perfumed island in the wide bed,
no longer his possession.

She was already undone, like long hair—
offered up, like fallen rain—
portioned out into a hundred pieces.

She was already root.

And when without warning the god
gripped her, and, agony in his voice,
spoke the words, *He has turned around—,*
she understood nothing and said softly: *Who?*

One Way to Varanasi

19 January 1999

As they wouldn't believe him dead,
we stripped the blanket off and let
the body in the bunk cool down.
The jeans and white t-shirt marked
him as one of us, but under the clack
and shudder of the wheels, earth
was calling back its blood and
the back of his ears and neck turned
grape-purple-blue. He was going
nowhere now. Along the straight
track Varanasi's platform hurtled
toward us. Each time the train's brake
squealed, fog gripped the window,
thick as muslin layers that, five
hours later, would wrap the body
into a tidy packet, neat as any
Pharaoh's, ready to load on a bicycle
cart and sealed with crimson wax.

Varanasi Morning

20 January 1999

Mist drifts above the river, masks
the other shore, softens what we try
to forget as the mass of water swings
past: clumsy tree trunks bob; gray
hump signals the body of a cow;
pale paper cup spinning.

She sits, her back to the bow,
my twenty-two-year-old daughter,
arms bare and lovely, sunglasses
drawn down like a shield.

We are tourists and mourners, at one
moment fixing the telephoto lens
on the man who dips his toothbrush
into polluted water, and at another
moving the camera's gaze to the tall
chimneys of the crematorium where late
last night the gauze-wrapped body
of our friend was changed, for eighty
rupees, into greasy smoke and lumps
of bone rattling in a clay pot.

Around her neck, the circlet of red
stones gleams luscious as the heap
of pomegranate seeds she pried
from their skin and gathered in a bowl:
our breakfast at the India Hotel, stuffed
parantha thick with oil, steaming cups
of tea, tang of curd, and those red seeds.

How to journey up from death? Tilt
of the head: it's okay. Her smooth
forehead: hard to enter light. Her hand
on the thwart: what is. Shadow
pressed gently on her throat, the dark
wedge her shirt makes, the red stones
like beads of jet now on her skin.

Her head turns toward shore and crumbling
palaces. Behind her, the Ganges slides.

The Greatcoat

Georgia O'Keeffe, 1920

Impermeable. I'm armored in black wool,
thick as his loden. He crouches at my feet

and his lens pays homage to the storm clouds
massed behind my head. The mannish hat

is my black halo, ringed by flinty gray.
I could be Jupiter contemplating what to strike,

or Juno blistering her way through his disguises
to the boy who hides behind the round glass eye.

But when he rises, I clutch collar to cheek,
duck nose into shelter. Fingers clench, the edge

of wool a ledge of bending rock. Shadows paint
seams on the plaster mask. Skin cracks, and the part

in my hair gapes wide. I must have shivered while
seconds tricked my eyes into that blur of falling.

What It Comes Down To

everything expands & contracts,
fills, rounds, quickens, shreds

garlic is the *sine qua non*

clouds are expert: they know
how to thin, how to release fingers,
how to watch love dissolve

emotional tears contain more protein

stingers of bees can be slid
out of skin, poison sac intact,
if one uses one's nail judiciously

excrement must be dealt with

not all the young are happy, nor
the old wise: 5% of the young are
wise; 2.6% of the old, happy

if grief is a tent, joy is no shelter

according to Queen Victoria who
experienced one & observed the other,
giving birth is harder than dying

nothing I've written is true

each of us is the man
in the Balthus painting,
carrying the plank

Black Bun

If Scotland had a Seamus Heaney, he'd have dug
you out of Jura's blackest bog—uncompromising

wedge of peat, pure darkness in a block—and made
you famous. But the Scots have kept you hidden. No

tea-towel image on the Royal Mile for you. You've
outdone trifle, oatcake, shortbread, haggis, scone,

in the race to be invisible. Each staggers to its cross,
leaves its face on the linen, while you live under

the radar, appearing only when the sun slips
so low it barely clears the horizon and hangs

there bitter. Across the land, from Stornoway
to Hawick, from Ballachulish to Auchtermuchty,

women roll out pastry, line the coffin-like tin, press
down batter that is nothing but currants, pepper,

milk, sugar, whisky, then lay the lid on tight.
On Hogmanay, you're cut and eaten, grained

and heavy, a mouth of prehistory that urges
us to look into death's shy gaze and offer her

a piece of black bun, ticket for the journey,
and then to swallow our own slice.

Bridge Steet Cemetery

Northampton, Massachusetts, 10 December 2001

for Agha Shahid Ali

frost-fog wraps wheelbarrow in flowers of ice

What keeps this light from pouring out as light?

his father lifts spade implacable weight as sand strikes wood

What keeps this light from pouring out?

in each poet's hand no words but grains

What keeps this light from pouring?

two skeins of geese row between snow and cloud

What keeps this light?

the imam prays "may this whiteness cleanse our hearts"

What keeps?

and tell us Shahid you who are so extravagantly wise

What keeps this light from pouring out as light?

Song

At night my mother is the washerwoman
who bleaches the clouds, and my father

the baker who kneads and shapes the hills,
my sister the fiddler for the waves' dance,

and my lost brother the carpenter who cobbles
a bed for the sun, a chair for the moon.

I hear them at their work, and my dreams
are ribbons that unravel and race to reach

them. The moon's sorrow undoes the day.
The chatter of sparrows undoes the night.

Words

When did I forget how to plowter, how
to be scunnert, how to look for foozle

under the bed? When, afraid of sounding
twee, did I stop saying wee? Who snatched

away douce and douchty? I lost my spurtle,
grew too proud to be wabbit, avoided any

kind of big stramash. Even when my Libra
soul pendulumed alarmingly, I didn't swither.

I quarreled with the Bens, sent the burns
into exile. Did they creep slowly off, little

gray mice looking for another home (no
sleekit rodents this side of the pond)?

How proper it all became, no screech
of pipes, no eightsome reels, no raucous

ceilidhs, no cailleachs with their thin white
hairs and whisperings, no burach spreading

out across the floor. Nuala sees her
language as a boat, a coracle to launch

in the bulrushes and send off to "some
Pharaoh's daughter." I saw mine as

something like a wart, a fart, a sneeze.
And, oh my lost darlings, I run after you

now, wrap treacherous arms round
you, dust you off, feed you kippers

from Loch Fyne and whisky from Islay,
then pin you on the page, as witness.

Glossary

Ah	I
auld	old
bairn	child
ben	hill; inside
braw	beautiful
bricht	bright
burach	mess
burn	stream
cailleach	old woman
ceilidh	informal concert
clanjamfrie	gang
clarty	dirty
disnae	doesn't
doon	down
douce	gentle
douchty	strong
foozle	dust bunnies
gie	give
girdle	variant of "griddle"
hauld	hold
hen	dear
Hogmanay	New Year's Eve
jalouse	imagine
masel	myself
mebbe	maybe
moonlicht	moonlight
neep	turnip
nicht	night
noo	now
o	of
oot	out
orright	all right
plowter	fiddle aimlessly
scunnert	disgusted
sleekit	smooth
smir	light drizzle
spaldered	spread out
spurtle	porridge stick
stramash	brouhaha
strathspey	slow dance

stravaig	wander
swither	hesitate
tae	to
tattie	potato
tawse	leather strap
thrums	purrs
wabbit	weakly exhausted
whaur	where
widdershins	anticlockwise

Notes

Many of these poems were written in memory of Alexander Wishart Edwards (1908-52) and Jean Fulton Edwards (1905-2004), loving parents.

"Witch Hazel in March" is dedicated to Li-Young Lee; "Ancestor Theory," to Sonia Sanchez; and "One Way to Varanasi," to the memory of Glenn Paterson.

PAGE 13 "ROCKFIELD PRIMARY SCHOOL"
Sir Walter Scott, "Lochinvar"

PAGE 20 "LIMINAL"
Thomas Wyatt, "They Flee from Me"; Gary Snyder, "How Poetry Comes to Me"

PAGE 27 "NEST OF THISTLES"
William Miller, "Willie Winkie"

PAGE 49 "FLOWERS À LA CARTE"
Hugh MacDiarmid, "The Little White Rose"

PAGE 52 "HAGGIS"
Robert Burns, "To a Haggis"

PAGE 72 "BRIDGE STREET CEMETERY"
Agha Shahid Ali, "The Purse Seiner *Atlantis*"

PAGE 74 "WORDS"
Nuala Ní Dhomhnaill, "The Language Issue," trans. Paul Muldoon

A Note on the Author

ANNIE BOUTELLE, born and raised in Scotland, was educated at the University of St. Andrews and New York University. Author of *Thistle and Rose: A Study of Hugh MacDiarmid's Poetry*, she teaches in the English Department at Smith College, where she founded the Poetry Center. She has published in various journals, including *The Georgia Review*, *The Green Mountains Review*, *The Hudson Review*, *Nimrod*, *Poet Lore*, and *Poetry*. Her first book of poems, based on the life of Celia Thaxter, is *Becoming Bone*. She lives with her husband in western Massachusetts.

A Note on the Prize

The Samuel French Morse Poetry Prize was established in 1983 by the Northeastern University Department of English in order to honor Professor Morse's distinguished career as teacher, scholar, and poet. The members of the prize committee are: Francis C. Blessington, Joseph deRoche, Victor Howes, Stuart Peterfreund, Guy Rotella, and Ellen Scharfenberg.